A Note From Rick Renner

I am on a personal quest to see a "revival of the Bible" so people can establish their lives on a firm foundation that will stand strong and endure the test as the end-time storm winds begin to intensify.

In order to experience a revival of the Bible in your personal life, it is important to take time each day to read, receive, and apply its truths to your life. James tells us that if we will continue in the perfect law of liberty — refusing to be forgetful hearers but determined to be doers — we will be blessed in our ways. As you watch or listen to the programs in this series and work through this corresponding study guide, I trust that you will search the Scriptures and allow the Holy Spirit to help you hear something new from God's Word that applies specifically to your life. I encourage you to be a doer of the Word that He reveals to you. Whatever the cost, I assure you — it will be worth it.

> Thy words were found, and I did eat them;
> and thy word was unto me the joy and rejoicing of mine heart:
> for I am called by thy name, O Lord God of hosts.
> — Jeremiah 15:16

Your brother and friend in Jesus Christ,

Rick Renner

The Stage of Faith

Copyright © 2021 by Rick Renner
8316 E. 73rd St.
Tulsa, Oklahoma 74133

Published by Rick Renner Ministries
www.renner.org

ISBN 13: 978-1-68031-861-6

eBook ISBN 13: 978-1-68031-862-3

How To Use
This Study Guide

This five-lesson study guide corresponds to *"The Stage of Faith" With Rick Renner* (Renner TV). Each lesson in this study guide covers a topic that is addressed during the program series, with questions and references supplied to draw you deeper into your own private study of the Scriptures on this subject.

To derive the most benefit from this study guide, consider the following:

First, watch or listen to the program prior to working through the corresponding lesson in this guide. (Programs can also be viewed at **renner.org** by clicking on the Media/Archives links.)

Second, take the time to look up the scriptures included in each lesson. Prayerfully consider their application to your own life.

Third, use a journal or notebook to make note of your answers to each lesson's Study Questions and Practical Application challenges.

Fourth, invest specific time in prayer and in the Word of God to consult with the Holy Spirit. Write down the scriptures or insights He reveals to you.

Finally, take action! Whatever the Lord tells you to do according to His Word, do it.

For added insights on this subject, it is recommended that you obtain Rick Renner's books *Build Your Foundation: Six Must-Have Beliefs for Constructing an Unshakable Christian Life*. You may also select from Rick's other available resources by placing your order at **renner.org** or by calling 1-800-742-5593.

TOPIC

Your Faith Will Put You Center Stage

SCRIPTURES

1. **Hebrews 10:32,33** — But call to remembrance the former days, in which, after ye were illuminated, ye endured a great fight of afflictions; partly, whilst ye were made a gazingstock both by reproaches and afflictions; and partly, whilst ye became companions of them that were so used.

2. **2 Peter 1:10** — Wherefore the rather, brethren, give diligence to make your calling and election sure....

GREEK WORDS

1. "but" — δὲ (*de*): an exclamatory point

2. "call to remembrance" — ἀναμιμνήσκω (*anamimnesko*): to recollect; to unbury, dust off, resurrect, and remember

3. "former" — πρότερον (*proteron*): former; before; earlier

4. "illuminated" — φωτίζω (*photidzo*): to lighten up, to shine, to illuminate; the impression of a brilliant flash of light that leaves a permanent and lasting impression

5. "endured" — ὑπομένω (*hupomeno*): to stay or abide; to remain in one's spot; to keep a position; to resolve to maintain territory gained; in a military sense, it pictures soldiers ordered to maintain their positions even in the face of opposition; to defiantly stick it out regardless of pressures mounted against it; staying power; hang-in-there power; the attitude that holds out, holds on, outlasts, perseveres, and hangs in there, never giving up, refusing to surrender to obstacles, and turning down every opportunity to quit; it pictures one who is under a heavy load but refuses to bend, break, or surrender because he is convinced that the territory, promise, or principle under assault rightfully belongs to him

6. "great" — πολλὴν (*pollen*): great in terms of quantity; many; substantial numbers

7. "fight" — ἄθλησις (*athlesis*): an athletic term that refers to the atti-
    tude and activities of a committed athlete; denotes athletic competi-
    tions or athletic games; can be translated as the word struggle; denotes
    a heroic act

8. "afflictions" — πάθημα (*pathema*): suffering; a strong emotional strug-
    gle; emotional or mental agony

9. "gazingstock" — θεατρίζω (*theatridzo*): theater; to observe, to watch,
    to study, to scrutinize, or to bring upon the stage for all to see; pictures
    spectators in the theater watching a scenario being played before
    them; on the edge of their seats, spectators wait for the actors to make
    a mistake or forget a line so they can scorn, ridicule, and make fun of
    him; it can be interpreted to bring on to the stage in order to scorn, to
    scoff at, to shame, sneer at, and to publicly humiliate; spectacle

10. "give diligence" — σπουδάζω (*spoudadzo*): to do something with
    eagerness; to do something with diligence; acting responsibly, quickly,
    and with attentiveness; one so diligent, excited and energetic, that he
    puts his whole heart into the principle or task before him

11. "calling" — κλῆσις (*klesis*): in the New Testament, it depicts a divine
    call; a special invitation given by God that must be accepted and
    embraced

12. "election" — ἐκλογή (*ekloge*): from ἐκλέγω (*eklego*), to call out, to
    select, to elect, or to choose; refers to individuals who were selected
    for a specific purpose; conveys the idea of the privilege and honor of
    being chosen; those being selected should look upon themselves as
    honored, esteemed, and respected; here it means chosen for a pre-
    planned outcome and conclusion

13. "sure" — βέβαιος (*bebaios*): authenticated, verified, guaranteed, estab-
    lished, made firm, concrete, sure, or steadfast; immoveable; a legal term
    used to depict the lengthy process involved that validated a document
    was trustworthy; if found trustworthy, the document bore authority

SYNOPSIS

The five lessons in this study on *The Stage of Faith* will focus on the
following topics:

• Your Faith Will Put You Center Stage

• Your Faith Will Cause People To Choose Sides

• Your Faith Will Bring You Attention

- Your Faith Will Bring Applause
- Your Faith Will Bring You Reward

The emphasis of this lesson:

When you make a declaration of faith, you end up center stage, and people buy a seat to watch and see if you're really going to do what you said you were going to do. God wants you to always remember what He called you to do and persevere to complete your faith assignment, regardless of the opposition that comes against you.

Located in Saint Petersburg, Russia, is the breathtaking Yusupov Palace, a residence that was enjoyed by the Yusupov family for five generations. Like their Romanov relatives, the Yusupovs were fabulously wealthy, owning three to six residences in the city of Saint Petersburg along with three large homes in Moscow and 57 estates in 16 provinces of Russia.

In addition to being very affluent, the Yusupovs were extremely talented musically. But because they were nobility, they were not allowed to perform on any public stage, which was very frustrating because they desperately wanted to perform. To overcome this dilemma, the Yusupov Palace featured a music room and an in-home theater that was amazing beyond description. On a regular basis, they would invite their friends, dignitaries, ambassadors, and even the Romanovs — their royal relatives — to come and view their performances.

As guests arrived, they entered the Yusupov Palace by way of a beautiful staircase and then made their way through several opulent rooms. Ladies were adorned in beautiful gowns, and men were donned with handsome attire for a fabulous evening. During these special events, the air was filled with great anticipation. Guests were excited about what they were going to see performed on the stage of the Yusupov in-home theater.

In a similar way, when a person makes a declaration of faith, it places them on an unseen stage, and the people around them begin to watch their lives play out to see if what they are believing for will actually come to pass.

Think about it. If you live your life on the sidelines, never doing anything significant, no one really takes note of your actions. On the other hand, the moment you say you're going to do something specific, it's as if people buy a ticket to watch the show. They're watching to see if you're going to make it through every scene of your performance. What's more, many of the spectators develop opinions as to whether or not you're going to stay on the stage and do what you said you're going to do or bail out. This is what the Bible tells us in Hebrews 10, which is what we will explore in these next five lessons.

Call to Remembrance the Former Days

In Hebrews 10:32 and 33, the Bible says, "But call to remembrance the former days, in which, after ye were illuminated, ye endured a great fight of afflictions; partly, whilst ye were made a gazingstock both by reproaches and afflictions; and partly, whilst ye became companions of them that were so used." Let's take a close look at the original Greek meaning of these passages, starting with verse 32.

First, notice the word "but." It is the Greek word *de*, which is *an exclamatory point*. By using this word, it is as if the writer of Hebrews is saying, "Hey, hey, hey! Stop! There's something you need to remember." It appears that the First-Century recipients of this letter were being tempted to walk away from their confession of faith and give up on their assignment. They had been waiting and waiting and were growing exhausted from the resistance they were experiencing.

The writer then said, "But call to remembrance the former days..." (Hebrews 10:32). The phrase "call to remembrance" is a translation of the Greek word *anamimnesko*, which means *to recollect; to unbury, dust off, resurrect, and remember*. The word "former" is the Greek word *proteron*, which means *former; before;* or *earlier*. Here, the writer was calling on these believers to stop everything they were doing — or were considering doing — and unbury, dust off, and resurrect the earlier, former days when they had been "illuminated."

This word "illuminated" is quite interesting. It is the Greek word *photidzo*, which means *to lighten up, to shine,* or *to illuminate*. It depicts the impression of *a brilliant flash of light that leaves a permanent and lasting impression*. This is the description of the day when you were walking with the Lord and suddenly you received a powerful revelation of truth. It may have been an eye-opening revelation from Scripture or something specific about the call of God on your life. That moment was so enlightening it left a permanent, lasting impression that transformed your life.

Unfortunately, usually after we're "illuminated" with a specific truth or assignment, life happens. Things get busy, we become distracted, and many times disappointments take place that snuff out the light of what God revealed. The dream that was once burning brightly inside of us becomes buried by the dirt of everyday life. This is what was happening to the First-Century Hebrew believers and why the writer told them to *call to remembrance the former days in which they were illuminated.*

Endure the Fight,
Refusing To Give Up or Give In

What's also interesting about Hebrews 10:32 is that the writer notes that after these believers were illuminated, they "…endured a great fight of afflictions." The word "endured" here is very important. It is a translation of the Greek word *hupomeno*, which means *to stay or abide; to remain in one's spot; to keep a position;* or *to resolve to maintain territory gained.* In a military sense, it pictures soldiers ordered to maintain their positions even in the face of opposition.

Moreover, the word *hupomeno* — translated here as "endured" — means *to defiantly stick it out regardless of pressures mounted against it.* It could be translated as *staying power; hang-in-there power; the attitude that holds out, holds on, outlasts, perseveres, and hangs in there, never giving up, refusing to surrender to obstacles, and turning down every opportunity to quit.* It pictures *one who is under a heavy load but refuses to bend, break, or surrender because he is convinced that the territory, promise, or principle under assault rightfully belongs to him.*

Again, the Bible says the Hebrew believers endured "a great fight of afflictions." The word "great" here is the Greek word *pollen*, which describes *something great in terms of quantity.* It can also indicate *many* or *substantial numbers.* These Hebrew believers were facing a *substantial number* of "fight of afflictions." The word "fight" in Greek is the word *athlesis*, which is an athletic term that refers to *the attitude and activities of a committed athlete.* Specifically, it denotes *athletic competitions or athletic games.* This word can be translated as the word *struggle*, and it denotes *a heroic act.*

This brings us to the word "afflictions," which is the Greek word *pathema*, and it describes *suffering.* This word could also be translated as *a strong emotional struggle* or *emotional or mental agony.* The truth is, the most difficult part of suffering is not what you feel in your body. It's what you experience in your mind and your emotions. When you're doing everything you know to do to "endure" (*hupomeno*) and not give up on what you believe God made real to you, you often encounter sarcasm and negativity from others, not to mention circumstances that appear to be the exact opposite of what you're believing for. It's in those moments that the mental and emotional anguish reaches an unbearable apex — almost like you're coming apart at the seams.

It is in those moments you have to make a decision that you're going to refuse to bend, refuse to break, and refuse to surrender to the pressure. Because you were "illuminated," you know deep in your spirit that what God has said is going to take place, so you reject every opportunity to quit.

Your Declaration of Faith
Makes You a 'Gazingstock' That Others Watch

Meanwhile, as you are enduring these great difficulties, the Bible says you — like the Hebrew believers in the First Century — become "...a gazing-stock both by reproaches and afflictions..." (Hebrews 10:34). This word "gazingstock" is the Greek word *theatridzo*, which is the word for a *theater*. It means *to observe, to watch, to study, to scrutinize, or to bring upon the stage for all to see*. It pictures spectators in the theater watching a scenario being played out before them. They're on the edge of their seats, like spectators waiting for the actors to make a mistake or forget a line so they can scorn, ridicule, and make fun of them.

This word *theatridzo* — translated here as "gazingstock" — can also be interpreted *to bring on to the stage in order to scorn, scoff at, shame, sneer at, and to publicly humiliate*. It is often translated as the word *spectacle*, which tells us that when you make a declaration of faith, you become a *big show*. It's as if people buy a seat to watch your performance and see if you actually do what you said God called you to do. Will you actually finish school and get your degree? Will you launch out into fulltime ministry and begin impacting people's lives? Will you start that business or write that book you said God told you to write?

Suddenly the people around you begin to say things like, "Do you think he'll do it? Did he really hear from God, or is what he's saying just a fantasy he made up?" This is how people respond — including some family members and friends. Like it or not, the moment you make a declaration of faith and step out in obedience and partner with God to see it become a reality, you become a "gazingstock" or a *theater* that people observe.

Well, if others are watching each scene of your life play out, why not give them something amazing to see? Every day, make it your aim to get up and give God glory in everything you do. Through the empowerment of the Holy Spirit, do something so magnificent that when you accomplish it, people will rise up and give you a standing ovation for succeeding. More importantly, when they see that you succeeded, it will encourage *them* to get up on the stage of faith and begin to perform their own assignment.

Make Your Calling and Election Sure

The apostle Peter touches on this idea in his second epistle. He said, "Wherefore the rather, brethren, give diligence to make your calling and election sure…" (2 Peter 1:10). The words "give diligence" are a translation of the Greek word *spoudadzo*, which means *to do something with eagerness* or *to do something with diligence*. It carries the idea of *acting responsibly, quickly, and with attentiveness*. It is the picture of one so diligent, excited and energetic, that he puts his whole heart into the task before him, making his "calling and election" sure.

The word "calling" in Second Peter 1:10 is the Greek word *klesis*. In the New Testament, this word depicts *a divine call* or *a special invitation given by God that must be accepted and embraced*. God wants you to act responsibly and attentively, pouring your energy and efforts into fulfilling your divine call and your "election." This word "election" is the Greek word *ekloge*, which is from the word *eklego*, meaning *to call out, to select, to elect, or to choose*. This refers to *individuals who were selected for a specific purpose*, and it conveys the idea of the privilege and honor of being chosen. Those being selected should look upon themselves as honored, esteemed, and respected. Here it means *chosen for a preplanned outcome and conclusion*.

Most assuredly, God has personally selected you to do something specific to bring Him glory. His will is for you to make it all the way to the end of your faith performance. That is why He instructs us to make our calling and election "sure." The word "sure" is the Greek word *bebaios*, and it means *authenticated, verified, guaranteed, established, made firm, concrete, sure, or steadfast*. It depicts something *immovable*. The word *bebaios* — translated here as "sure" — was a legal term used to depict the lengthy process involved that validated if a document was trustworthy. If found trustworthy, the document bore authority.

Through Peter, the Holy Spirit is telling us, "Hey! Before you get on the stage of faith, you need to first make sure that what you're about to do is what you're called to do. Once your calling and election are *authenticated* and *verified* — do it!

In our next lesson, we will examine a passage in First Corinthians 4 and see how your walk of faith will cause people to choose sides.

STUDY QUESTIONS

> Study to shew thyself approved unto God, a workman that needeth
> not to be ashamed, rightly dividing the word of truth.
> — 2 Timothy 2:15

1. Take some time to carefully reflect on the meaning of the word "endured" — the Greek word *hupomeno*. What new insights is the Holy Spirit showing you about what it means to *endure*?

2. Just like the early Hebrew church, many others in Scripture had a *photidzo* moment where their calling was clearly illuminated and confirmed by God. Which ones can you think of? (*HINT*: Take a look at these passages for a few of their stories: Esther 4:14, First Samuel 3, First Samuel 16:1-13, Luke 1:26-38, and Acts 9:1-18.)

3. Remember the story of Joseph in the Old Testament? If anyone truly understood the words *hupomeno* (enduring, defiantly sticking it out, refusing to quit) and *pathema* (suffering, mental/emotional agony), Joseph did (see Genesis 37 and 39-41). After going through so much unfair treatment and countless disappointments in pursuit of his divine calling (*klesis*), what was his conclusion after finally seeing God's plan for his life come to fruition (see Genesis 45:4-8)? How does this give you hope for your own future?

PRACTICAL APPLICATION

> But be ye doers of the word, and not hearers only,
> deceiving your own selves.
> — James 1:22

1. Can you remember a *photidzo* moment in your life? A time when you were "illuminated" and something you had never seen before was brought into the light of your understanding, and it changed your

perspective? Briefly share one such situation and how it transformed your life.

2. Like the First-Century Hebrew believers, are you being tempted to walk away from your confession of faith and give up on your assignment? Have you been waiting and waiting and grown exhausted from the resistance you've been experiencing? Briefly share what you've been enduring. How is this lesson encouraging you to persevere in your calling?

TOPIC

Your Faith Will Cause People To Choose Sides

SCRIPTURES

1. **1 Corinthians 4:9,11-13** — ...For we are made a spectacle unto the world, and to angels, and to men. Even unto this present hour we both hunger, and thirst, and are naked, and are buffeted, and have no certain dwellingplace; and labour, working with our own hands: being reviled, we bless; being persecuted, we suffer it: being defamed, we intreat: we are made as the filth of the world, and are the offscouring of all things unto this day.

GREEK WORDS

1. "spectacle" — θέατρον (*theatridzo*): theater; to observe, to watch, to study, to scrutinize, or to bring upon the stage for all to see; pictures spectators in the theater watching a scenario being played before them; on the edge of their seats, spectators wait for the actors to make a mistake or forget a line so they can scorn, ridicule him, and make fun of him; it can be interpreted to bring on to the stage in order to scorn, to scoff at, to shame, sneer at, and to publicly humiliate; spectacle

2. "world" — κόσμος (*kosmos*): conveys ideas of order and arrangement; can describe the universe because, although huge, diverse, and ever-expanding, the universe is a perfectly ordered and arranged

system; describes society because it is a system that possesses order and arrangement; also carries with it the ideas of culture, fashion, and sophistication

3. "angels" — ἄγγελος (*angelos*): plural, angels; a word that describes either a human messenger or an angel; one who is sent on a special mission; one who is dispatched to perform a specific assignment; often used to denote a delegate or dignitary; it can picture the role of a pastor; a messenger of God; here, heavenly angels

4. "men" — ἄνθρωπος (*anthropos*): plural, men; depicts the entire human race, both men and women, and all ages

5. "hunger" — πεινάω (*peinao*): to be desperately hungry; to earnestly seek to satisfy physical hunger

6. "thirst" — διψάω (*dipsao*): to be hungry from a lack of food, or to be thirsty from a lack of drink

7. "naked" — γυμνητεύω (*gumneteuo*): to be poorly or ill-dressed

8. "buffeted" — κολαφίζω (*kolaphidzo*): to strike with the fist; used to picture a person who is violently beaten; a beating by knuckles or fists; fists as weapons of abuse; maltreatment

9. "no certain dwelling place" — ἀστατέω (*astateo*): to wander about; to rove without a settled place to live; to have no certain dwelling-place; a roaming life that is physically unsettled; no status

10. "labour" — κοπιάω (*kopiao*): the hardest and most wearisome kind of labor; toil; one who gives everything to a project or assignment; one who strives and works with every fiber of his being; typifies work that may be wearisome, exhausting; the hardest kind of labor; applies to physical, mental, or spiritual effort

11. "reviled" — λοιδορέω (*loidoreo*): crude, coarse, vulgar, abusive language; to speak abusively, to insult someone, or to speak words that are crude and vile; verbal abuse

12. "bless" — εὐλογέω (*eulogeo*): to speak good words; to invoke blessings

13. "persecuted" — διώκω (*dioko*): to hunt, to chase, or to pursue; to persecute; it denoted the actions of a hunter who followed after an animal in order to apprehend, to capture to kill it; like a hunter, to strategically follow after an object, principle, person, or reward until it is captured

14. "suffer" — ἀνέχομαι (*anechomai*): to endure; to put up with; to be tolerant, especially of others

15. "defamed" — δυσφημία (*dusphemia*): to slander, to slur, to smear, or to vilify; to maliciously malign someone's good name; depicts one who deliberately does a hatchet job on someone's integrity, character, or name; an attack carried out with the purposeful intention of damaging someone's reputation in the eyes of others; malicious and nasty character attacks; defamation

16. "intreat" — παρακαλέω (*parakaleo*): to urge, beseech, plead, beg, pray; pictures one who has come closely alongside of another person for the sake of speaking to him, consoling him, comforting him, or assisting him with instruction, counsel, or advice; in ancient times, depicted military leaders who came alongside their troops to urge, exhort, beseech, beg, and plead with them to stand tall and face their battles bravely

17. "filth" — περικάθαρμα (*perikatharma*): compound of περι (*peri*) and καθαίρω (*kathairo*); the word περι (*peri*) means around, and the word καθαίρω (*kathairo*) means to cleanse or to purify; depicts the removal of disgusting grime; one of the lowest, crudest derogatory statements that could be made about someone; used to describe low-level people in society, such as criminals deemed unworthy to live; it was believed if a city had a chain of bad fortune, public officials should give the order for the "filth" of society — low-level criminals — to be rounded up and publicly sacrificed, and that if this societal scum could be exterminated, it could reverse a city's bad fortune

18. "world" — κόσμος (*kosmos*): conveys ideas of order and arrangement; can describe the universe because, although huge, diverse, and ever-expanding, the universe is a perfectly ordered and arranged system; describes society because it is a system that possesses order and arrangement; also carries with it the ideas of culture, fashion, and sophistication

19. "offscouring" — περίψημα (*peripsema*): wiped-off filth; filth that is scrubbed and rubbed off and removed; depicts the ferocious process required to remove filth and grime; Romans and Greeks frequently looked for those they could blame for society's problems and ills, and they regularly pointed their fingers at low-level criminals — the so-called "scum of the earth" — and accused them of bringing bad luck on their populations; such people were viewed as bad omens that needed to be stamped out and eliminated, so from time to time, public officials gave the order for low-level people, criminals, and societal "scum" to be rounded up and executed, especially in times of plague,

war, famine, or other catastrophes; they believed that scrubbing out this scum from society would put an end to their bad luck

SYNOPSIS

As we noted in Lesson 1, the Yusupov Palace in Saint Petersburg, Russia, was simply fabulous. The Yusupov family lived there for 25 years, and today it remains in its original condition, unscathed even by the Bolshevik Revolution of 1917. This family was extremely talented but was banned from performing on a public stage because they were royalty. To overcome this challenge, the Yusupovs built an in-home theater in which they performed on a regular basis, inviting their friends, dignitaries, and even their royal relatives, the Romanovs, to watch.

When guests arrived, they made their way up the grand staircase and into the exquisite ballroom. From the ballroom, they turned and were escorted into the great banquet hall, which was surrounded by majestic columns and stunning chandeliers that appeared to be made of gold. The startling truth is they are actually made of paper maché. It was in this room that great and formal festivities and banquets took place. The Yusupovs even held many charity events here to raise money for the destitute and the poor. Today this room is used primarily as a concert hall.

Once the guests were led through the banquet hall, they then passed into the luxurious art gallery and finally made their way into the theater. With great anticipation, attendees quickly took their seats and waited for the show to begin. It's interesting to note that just as people loved to attend performances then, they love to attend performances now — including the performance of those who make a declaration of faith.

As we noted in our first lesson, when you step out in faith to do something you believe God called you to do, your life becomes a theater, and you are placed on center stage. It's as if people buy a seat to the show to see how well you're going to do. Therefore, since they have come to watch you, why not aim to give them the best performance possible so they can really see how faith works.

The emphasis of this lesson:

When we step out in faith to do what God has called us to do, the Bible says society, the angels in Heaven, and the entire human race begin watching to see how well we perform. In the process, we sometimes ex-

perience hunger, thirst, nakedness, and harsh treatment. Through it all, we are to bless our enemies and encourage each other to stay in the fight.

Paul's Overview of the Conditions He and His Team Endured

Just as the writer of Hebrews told his First-Century readers that walking by faith places them on a stage, the apostle Paul made a similar declaration to the believers in Corinth. We find this recorded in his first letter to the Corinthians in which He said:

> …For we are made a spectacle unto the world, and to angels, and to men.
>
> Even unto this present hour we both hunger, and thirst, and are naked, and are buffeted, and have no certain dwellingplace;
>
> And labour, working with our own hands: being reviled, we bless; being persecuted, we suffer it:
>
> Being defamed, we intreat: we are made as the filth of the world, and are the offscouring of all things unto this day.
>
> 1 Corinthians 4:9,11-13

Let's take some time to carefully examine each of these four verses and the original Greek meaning of several important words.

We Are a 'Spectacle'

Paul begins by saying, "…For we are made a spectacle unto the world, and to angels, and to men" (1 Corinthians 4:9). Notice the word "spectacle." It is the Greek word *theatridzo* — the very same word we saw in Hebrews 10:33 that is translated as "gazingstock." It is the Greek word for a *theater*, and it means *to observe, to watch, to study, to scrutinize, or to bring upon the stage for all to see.* The use of this word tells us that when you accept God's call to do something by faith, you immediately leave the shadows of the private sector and are thrust onto the public stage.

This word *theatridzo* — translated here as "spectacle" — pictures spectators in the theater watching a scenario being played out before them. The word *theatridzo* can also be interpreted *to bring on to the stage in order to scorn, to scoff at, to shame, sneer at, and to publicly humiliate.* Spectators are on the edge of their seats waiting for the actors to make a mistake or forget a line so they can scorn, ridicule him, and make fun of him.

One would think that the people watching would applaud and praise us for having the guts to step out and attempt to do something special. But it seems that instead of cheers, the onlookers provide jeers — voicing criticism and cynicism over every mistake we make. Who are these spectators watching us? Paul categorized them into three groups: the world, angels, and men.

The World is Watching. The Greek word for "world" here is *kosmos*, which conveys ideas of *order and arrangement*. It can be used to describe *the universe* because, although huge, diverse, and ever-expanding, the universe is a perfectly ordered and arranged system. In this verse, however, the word *kosmos* — world — describes *society* because it is a system that possesses order and arrangement. This word also carries with it the notions of *culture, fashion,* and *sophistication.*

Angels Are Watching. The word "angels" is the Greek word *angelos,* and here it is plural, denoting a whole host of heavenly *angels.* In the New Testament, this word can describe either *a human messenger* or *an angel.* It is *one who is sent on a special mission; one who is dispatched to perform a specific assignment.* The word *angelos* is often used to denote *a delegate* or *dignitary.* It can even picture *the role of a pastor,* which is what we see in Christ's message to the seven major churches in Revelation 2 and 3. Here in First Corinthians 4:9, it describes *heavenly angels.*

Men Are Watching. The word "men" in this verse is the plural form of the Greek word *anthropos,* which depicts *the entire human race, both men and women, and all ages.* Thus, when we step out in faith to do what God has asked us to do, the Bible says society, the angels in Heaven, and the entire human race of men and women symbolically buy a ticket to sit and watch how well we perform on the stage of faith.

Walking By Faith Can Bring Challenges of Hunger, Thirst, Nakedness, and Buffeting

The apostle Paul went on to say, "Even unto this present hour we both hunger, and thirst, and are naked, and are buffeted, and have no certain dwellingplace" (1 Corinthians 4:11). This verse provides a snapshot of what Paul and his associates were facing.

For instance, take the word "hunger." It is the Greek word *peinao*, which means *to be desperately hungry* or *to earnestly seek to satisfy physical hunger*. The word "thirst" in Greek is *dipsao*, and it means *to be hungry from a lack of food*, or *to be thirsty from a lack of drink*.

In addition to being hungry and thirsty, Paul said they were "naked" at times. This is a translation of the word *gumneteuo*, which means *to be poorly or ill-dressed*. Next, Paul said they were "buffeted," which is a translation of the Greek word *kolaphidzo*, meaning *to strike with the fist*. This word was used to picture *a person who is violently beaten by knuckles or fists*. It depicts *fists as weapons of abuse* and is also the word for *maltreatment*.

The fourth condition Paul said they were dealing with is that they had "no certain dwelling place." This phrase is a translation of the word *astateo*, which means *to wander about; to rove without a settled place to live*. It can also mean *to have no certain dwelling-place* or describe *a roaming life that is physically unsettled*. This word *astateo* — translated here as "no certain dwelling place" — is from where we get the expression *to have no status*.

Like Paul and the First-Century believers, when we begin to walk out our faith assignment, not everyone will rejoice. There will be people who come against us, challenging circumstances to overcome, and harassing attacks from the devil and his demonic forces, all designed to de-platform us from the stage of faith. Satan knows that if you do what God has told you to do, there will be a ripple effect from your obedience that will change the lives of others. Therefore, he will do everything in his power to prevent you from fulfilling your God-assignment.

When Reviled and Persecuted, We Are To 'Suffer' It and Bless Others

To all this Paul added, "And [we] labour, working with our own hands: being reviled, we bless; being persecuted, we suffer it" (1 Corinthians 4:12). The word "labour" here is a form of the Greek word *kopiao*, which describes *the hardest and most wearisome kind of labor* or *toil*. It depicts *one who gives everything to a project or assignment; one who strives and works with every fiber of his being*. It typifies *work that may be wearisome or exhausting; the hardest kind of labor*. This word *kopiao* — translated here as "labour" — applies to physical, mental, or spiritual effort.

It's thought-provoking that even though Paul and his co-laborers were working as hard as they possibly could, performing the faith assignment God had given with every fiber of their being, the Bible says others "reviled" them. In Greek, the old *King James* word "reviled" is the word *loidoreo*, which describes *crude, coarse, vulgar, abusive language*. It means *to speak abusively, to insult someone, or to speak words that are crude and vile.* Essentially, it is *verbal abuse.*

Even though they were reviled, Paul said, "We bless." The word "bless" is the Greek word *eulogeo*, which means *to speak good words* or *to invoke blessings.* It is from where we get the word *eulogy.* In spite of being verbally abused, Paul encouraged believers to use their mouths to begin to speak the blessings of God on their critics.

In addition to being reviled, Paul said they were also "persecuted." In Greek, this is a form of the old hunting term *dioko*, which means *to hunt, to chase, or to pursue.* This word denoted *the actions of a hunter who followed after an animal in order to apprehend, to capture,* or *to kill it.* It is the picture of a hunter strategically following after an object, principle, person, or reward until it is captured. This word *dioko* indicates that there is nothing accidental about persecution; it is deliberate and intentional.

As they were being hunted like animals, Paul said they did "suffer it." In Greek, the word "suffer" is the word *anechomai*, and it means *to endure; to put up with;* or *to be tolerant, especially of others.* Basically, Paul is saying that when people revile and persecute us — being verbally abusive, spewing negativity, and trying to entrap us — we are to endure it by God's strength. The fact that He has called us on the stage of faith to do something amazing means that He Himself will empower us to perform it — if we will ask Him.

In the Midst of Harsh Treatment We Are To Encourage One Another Not To Give Up

In First Corinthians 4:13, Paul continued to describe the opposition they were facing and how they were responding to it. He said, "Being defamed, we intreat: we are made as the filth of the world, and are the offscouring of all things unto this day."

The word "defamed" in Greek is *dusphemia*, which means *to slander, to slur, to smear, or to vilify, to maliciously malign someone's good name.* This word depicts *one who deliberately does a hatchet job on someone's integrity, character, or name; an attack carried out with the purposeful intention of damaging someone's reputation in the eyes of others.* This word *dusphemia* — translated here as "defamed" — could also be translated as *malicious and nasty character attacks*; it is the Greek word for *defamation.*

Amidst the onslaught of these attacks, Paul said, "We intreat." This word "intreat" is the Greek word *parakaleo*, which means *to urge, beseech, plead, beg, or pray.* It is used many times throughout the New Testament, and it pictures *one who has come closely alongside of another person for the sake of speaking to him, consoling him, comforting him, or assisting him with instruction, counsel, or advice.* In ancient times, it depicted military leaders who came alongside their troops to urge, exhort, beseech, beg, and plead with them to stand tall and face their battles bravely. Paul's insertion of this word lets us know that when people came against them to vilify, slander, and smear their reputations, believers would come alongside each other to encourage one another to be brave, stand tall, and stay in the fight.

What else did Paul say they were experiencing? In First Corinthians 4:13 he declared, "…We are made as the filth of the world…." The word "filth" here is the Greek word *perikatharma*, which is a compound of the words *peri* and *kathairo.* The word *peri* means *around,* and the word *kathairo* means *to cleanse* or *to purify.* When these words are compounded to form *perikatharma*, it depicts *the removal of disgusting grime.* This word became one of the lowest, crudest derogatory statements that could be made about someone. So much so that it was used to describe low-level people in society, such as criminals deemed unworthy to live. It was believed if a city had a chain of bad fortune, public officials should give the order for the "filth" of society — low-level criminals — to be rounded up and publicly sacrificed, and that if this societal scum could be exterminated, it could reverse a city's bad fortune.

Along with being viewed as the filth of the world, believers were also perceived as the "offscouring of all things." In Greek, the word "offscouring" is *peripsema*, and it describes *the wiped-off filth* or *filth that is scrubbed and rubbed off and removed.* It depicts *the ferocious process required to remove filth and grime.* Romans and Greeks frequently looked for those they could blame for society's problems and ills, and they regularly pointed their fingers at low-level criminals — the so-called "scum of the earth" — and accused them of bringing bad luck on their populations. Such people were viewed as bad omens that needed to be stamped out and eliminated.

So from time to time, public officials gave the order for low-level people, criminals, and societal "scum" to be rounded up and executed — especially in times of plague, war, famine, or other catastrophes. They believed that scrubbing out this scum from society would put an end to their bad luck.

Paul's choice to use the word *peripsema* — translated here as "offscouring" — was very pointed. It was the same as him saying, "While we're out doing the will of God trying to help people, many in society look at us like we are filth and the offscouring of all things. And because we appear as disgusting, we should be eliminated. They're trying to rub us out for the sole reason that we're staying on the stage of faith doing what God has told us to do."

How Should You Respond to All This?

Now Paul doesn't tell us these things to scare us, but to prepare us for what we may have to deal with when God calls us to step out on the stage of faith and carry out a divine assignment. Whatever happens, **never forget that God promises to never leave your side** (*see* Hebrews 13:5,6). So don't let anyone's harsh response push you off the stage. Receive the power of the Holy Spirit, and He will enable you to give the best performance you can. And when you make it all the way to the end and fulfill your assignment, the same people who were cynical and critical will stand up and give you a round of applause.

As you humbly submit to the will of God, your life will have a rippling effect. That is, if you do what God has called you to do, it will encourage others to move from being a spectator to being a participant. They, too, will get out of their seats and take to the stage of faith to accomplish what God has placed in their heart.

In our next lesson, we will look at how living in faith will also bring you attention.

STUDY QUESTIONS

> Study to shew thyself approved unto God, a workman that needeth
> not to be ashamed, rightly dividing the word of truth.
> — 2 Timothy 2:15

1. Knowing that the world around us, the angels in heaven, and all of humanity are watching our lives, how should we live day in and day out? (Consider Hebrews 12:1,2.) Where should we keep our focus so that we can endure (*see* Philippians 2:5-11)?

2. It can be overwhelming to think of navigating pain and persecution, but thank God He doesn't expect or ask us to do it alone. In what specific ways does He promise to help us through hard times? Consider these verses:

   - **Philippians 2:12,13**
   - **Isaiah 43:1-3; 41:10-16**
   - **1 Corinthians 10:13**
   - **Hebrews 13:5,6**

PRACTICAL APPLICATION

> But be ye doers of the word, and not hearers only,
> deceiving your own selves.
> —James 1:22

1. Paul said that when we're mistreated, we need to respond with kindness and even blessings (*eulogeo*) — praying for those that slander us. And we are able to do this by the power of God's Spirit living in us. What are some practical ways we can respond out of love to people who cause us pain? (Consider Jesus' words in Luke 6:27-38 and Matthew 5:38-48 for some specific ideas.)

2. At some point, we will all come to a place where people will say and do hurtful things to us because we've chosen to follow Christ. How did Peter say we should respond to such harsh treatment (*see* 1 Peter 4:12-14)? What words of hope did Jesus give us to hold on to in Matthew 5:10-16 and Luke 6:22,23?

TOPIC

Your Faith Will Bring You Attention

SCRIPTURES

1. **Hebrews 10:32,33** — But call to remembrance the former days, in which, after ye were illuminated, ye endured a great fight of afflictions; partly, whilst ye were made a gazingstock both by reproaches and afflictions; and partly, whilst ye became companions of them that were so used.

2. **2 Corinthians 1:8-10** — For we would not, brethren, have you ignorant of our trouble which came to us in Asia, that we were pressed out of measure, above strength, insomuch that we despaired even of life: But we had the sentence of death in ourselves, that we should not trust in ourselves, but in God which raiseth the dead: Who delivered us from so great a death, and doth deliver: in whom we trust that he will yet deliver us.

GREEK WORDS

1. "but" — **δὲ** (*de*): an exclamatory point

2. "call to remembrance" — **ἀναμιμνήσκω** (*anamimnesko*): to recollect; to unbury, dust off, resurrect, and remember

3. "former" — **πρότερον** (*proteron*): former; before; earlier

4. "illuminated" — **φωτίζω** (*photidzo*): to lighten up, to shine, to illuminate; the impression of a brilliant flash of light that leaves a permanent and lasting impression

5. "endured" — **ὑπομένω** (*hupomeno*): to stay or abide; to remain in one's spot; to keep a position; to resolve to maintain territory gained; in a military sense, it pictures soldiers ordered to maintain their positions even in the face of opposition; to defiantly stick it out regardless of pressures mounted against it; staying power; hang-in-there power; the attitude that holds out, holds on, outlasts, perseveres, and hangs in there, never giving up, refusing to surrender to obstacles, and turning down every opportunity to quit; it pictures one who is under a heavy load but refuses to bend, break, or surrender because he is convinced

that the territory, promise, or principle under assault rightfully belongs to him

6. "great" — πολλὴν (*pollen*): great in terms of quantity; many; substantial numbers

7. "fight" — ἄθλησις (*athlesis*): an athletic term that refers to the attitude and activities of a committed athlete; denotes athletic competitions or athletic games; can be translated as the word struggle; denotes a heroic act

8. "afflictions" — πάθημα (*pathema*): suffering; a strong emotional struggle; emotional or mental agony

9. "gazingstock" — θεατρίζω (*theatridzo*): theater; to observe, to watch, to study, to scrutinize, or to bring upon the stage for all to see; pictures spectators in the theater watching a scenario being played before them; on the edge of their seats, spectators wait for the actors to make a mistake or forget a line so they can scorn, ridicule him, and make fun of him; it can be interpreted to bring on to the stage in order to scorn, to scoff at, to shame, sneer at, and to publicly humiliate; spectacle

10. "reproaches" — ὀνειδισμός (*oneidismos*): insults; language intended to injury, harm, hurt, or damage; words that damage one's reputation; to be verbally abusive; pictures what people do to others

11. "afflictions" — θλῖψις (*thlipsis*): affliction; tribulation; trouble; great pressure; crushing pressure; suffocating pressure; a horribly tight, life-threatening squeeze; to suffocate; to bully; the brunt of society; pressure to conform; a horribly tight, life-threatening squeeze; a situation so difficult it causes one to feel stressed, squeezed, pressured, or even crushed

12. "ignorant" — ἀγνοέω (*agnoeo*): ignorant; uninformed of the facts

13. "trouble" — θλῖψις (*thlipsis*): affliction; tribulation; trouble; great pressure; crushing pressure; suffocating pressure; a horribly tight, life-threatening squeeze; to suffocate; to bully; the brunt of society; pressure to conform; a horribly tight, life-threatening squeeze; a situation so difficult it causes one to feel stressed, squeezed, pressured, or even crushed

14. "pressed out of measure" — ὑπερβάλλω (*huperballo*): something that is above and beyond what is normal; exceeding or surpassing; pictures an archer who aims his arrow at the bullseye, but shoots way over the top; depicts something beyond the range of anything considered normal; something unparalleled

15. "above strength" — **ὑπὲρ δύναμιν** (*huper dunamin*): an experience way beyond one's power and abilities to endure or to overcome

16. "weighed down" — **βαρέω** (*bareo*): to weigh down; to overload; from **βάρος** (*baros*), depicting a weight that is heavy or crushing; a crushing weight; could refer to a physical problem, circumstantial problem, or spiritual problem; a burden too heavy to carry alone; if one attempts to carry it alone, it would be crushing to bear

17. "despaired" — **ἐξαπορέομαι** (*exaporeomai*): no way out; inescapable; describes one who feels trapped, caught, up against a wall, pinned down, and hence, utterly hopeless

18. "sentence" — **ἀπόκριμα** (*apokrima*): a judicial rendering; a judicial decision; a final outcome; a final verdict

SYNOPSIS

In the previous lessons, we have noted that the Yusupov family was extremely talented and loved to perform. But because they were royalty, they were not permitted to perform on a public stage. Therefore, they built their own private theater in their Saint Petersburg palace and held frequent performances for friends, dignitaries, and members of their family, which included the renowned Romanovs.

Guests that attended the Yusupov's performances would make their way through the ball room, the great banquet hall, and then be escorted through a series of five rooms that formed the family art gallery. At one time, this gallery included 1,100 pieces of priceless art and was quite an impressive display of wealth and power for those who viewed it.

From the art gallery, attendees entered the Yusupov's in-home theater, which was simply remarkable. It featured multiple balconies and marble steps that led to the main-floor seating. Altogether, this theater could accommodate up to 180 people. And on the small, private stage down front, members of the Yusupov family — as well as celebrated singers and musical artists such as Chopin — gave many memorable performances.

As we have noted in our previous lessons, when you step out in faith to do something for God, your faith places you on a stage, and people buy tickets to sit and watch you perform. They're looking to see if you're serious about what you said. They're listening to your every word and watching every move you make to see if you will accomplish the assignment God gave you. Indeed, when you are on the stage of faith, you are going to get lots of attention.

The emphasis of this lesson:

As Paul performed on the stage of faith, he experienced overwhelming, crushing pressure. The trouble was so far beyond his ability to endure he thought for sure that he would die. But he learned to put all his trust in God to deliver him, and God came through!

A Review of Hebrews 10:32

In Lesson 1, we focused on what the writer of Hebrews spoke to his First-Century readers toward the end of the tenth chapter. In an effort to encourage and bring hope to these believers, he said:

> **But call to remembrance the former days, in which, after ye were illuminated, ye endured a great fight of afflictions.**
> **— Hebrews 10:32**

We saw that the very first word — the word "but" — is the Greek word *de*, which is actually *an exclamatory point*. It is as if the writer is raising his voice and saying, "Hey, wait a minute! Hold on!" He was trying to capture the full attention of his readers that were extremely downtrodden and discouraged from the opposition they had been facing. They had continued to faithfully do what God had called them to do and were believing He would move on their behalf, but they still had not seen any answers to their prayers. To this the writer said…

"Call to remembrance" – These words are a translation of the Greek word *anamimnesko*, which means *to recollect; to unbury, dust off, resurrect, and remember*. Apparently, there was something of great value in their past that had become buried through the busyness and challenges of life. What was it?

"The former days" – The word "former" in Greek is the word *proteron*, which describes *something former; before; or earlier*. Specifically, the writer of Hebrews was urging believers to remember the former days when they were…

"Illuminated" – This word is from the Greek word *photidzo*, which means *to lighten up, to shine,* or *to illuminate*. The word *photidzo* is from where we get the word *photograph*, and it describes *the impression of a brilliant flash of light that leaves a permanent and lasting impression*. We might call this *a* *revelation.* This is what the writer of Hebrews was imploring his readers to remember — those moments in their past when the Holy Spirit had spoken to their hearts and made the truth come alive. That instant was like a brilliant flash of light that burned a lasting impression on them, and they were never the same again. Can you remember any *photidzo* moments in your life? God wants you to resurrect them, dust them off, and keep them in front of you.

The writer of Hebrews went on to describe the former days as a time when his readers had "...endured a great fight of afflictions" (Hebrews 10:32).

"Endured" – This is the Greek word *hupomeno*, which means *to stay or abide*; *to remain in one's spot*; *to keep a position*; or *to resolve to maintain territory gained*. In a military sense, it pictures soldiers ordered to maintain their positions even in the face of opposition. It means *to defiantly stick it out regardless of pressures mounted against it*. It could also be translated as *staying power* or *hang-in-there power*. It is *the attitude that holds out, holds on, outlasts, perseveres, and hangs in there, never giving up, refusing to surrender to obstacles, and turning down every opportunity to quit*. When opportunities to quit arise — and they certainly will — you have to reject them by the power of the Holy Spirit.

Furthermore, this word *hupomeno* — translated here as "endured" — pictures *one who is under a heavy load but refuses to bend, break, or surrender because he is convinced that the territory, promise, or principle under assault rightfully belongs to him*. The use of this word tells us that when you received an illumination from God, you have to make a decision to maintain it or you could lose it when the "great fight of afflictions" comes against you.

"Great fight of afflictions" – The word "great" in Hebrews 10:32 is the Greek word *pollen*, which means *great in terms of quantity*. It could also be translated as *many* as it describes *substantial numbers*. The word "fight" is the Greek word *athlesis*, which is an athletic term that refers to *the attitude and activities of a committed athlete*. It denotes *athletic competitions or athletic games* and can be translated as the word *struggle*. Moreover, this word *athlesis* — translated here as "fight" — depicts *a heroic act*.

Paul described this great fight as one of "afflictions." In Greek, this word "afflictions" is the word *pathema*, which could be translated as *suffering*. It describes *a strong emotional struggle* or *emotional or mental agony*. When you are in the midst of the fight, your physical body can endure a great deal. In contrast, what you come up against mentally and emotionally may be the most difficult thing you face. The cynicism, sarcasm, and negativity of the people who are watching you — not to mention the onslaught of satanic assaults against your mind — can become extremely difficult to bear.

Please understand, the devil won't just attack you once. He will come against you again and again, manipulating people and circumstances in an attempt to push you out of your place of faith and destroy you. Why? It's because the devil hates people who are illuminated and walking in faith. Illuminated people help bring illumination to others. They are a major threat to his kingdom, and he will fight them at every turn. That is why you must decide to stay on the stage of faith, holding tightly to what God told you until it becomes a reality.

We Become a 'Gazingstock' by 'Reproaches and Afflictions'

The writer of Hebrews went on to say, "…Ye were made a gazingstock both by reproaches and afflictions; and partly, whilst ye became companions of them that were so used" (Hebrews 10:33).

We've noted that the word "gazingstock" is the Greek word *theatridzo*, which is from where we get the word *theater*. It means *to observe, to watch, to study, to scrutinize, or to bring upon the stage for all to see*. It pictures spectators in the theater watching a scenario being played before them. They are on the edge of their seats, waiting for the actors to make a mistake or forget a line so they can scorn, ridicule, and make fun of them. This word *theatridzo* can also be interpreted *to bring on to the stage in order to scorn, to scoff at, to shame, sneer at, and to publicly humiliate*.

Friend, when you get a revelation of truth or a divine assignment from God and you step out in faith to fulfill it, you leave the private sector and become a public spectacle — a "gazingstock." It is as if people buy a ticket to sit and watch you perform, all the while critiquing your every move.

Notice the Bible goes on to say you become a "gazingstock" "…both by reproaches and afflictions…" (Hebrews 10:33). The word "reproaches" is the Greek word *oneidismos*, which describes *insults* or *language intended to injure, harm, hurt, or damage*. It denotes *words that damage one's reputation*. It carries the idea of being *verbally abusive* and is *a picture of what people do to others*.

The word "afflictions," on the other hand, describes what life does. In this verse, it is the Greek word *thlipsis*, which can be translated as *affliction*, *tribulation*, or *trouble*. It depicts *great pressure; crushing pressure; suffocating pressure;* or *a horribly tight, life-threatening squeeze*. It can also mean *to suffocate* or *to bully* and denotes *the brunt of society* and *pressure to conform*. Again, it is *a horribly tight, life-threatening squeeze; a situation so difficult it causes one to feel stressed, squeezed, pressured, or even crushed*.

The use of the words "reproaches" and "afflictions" tells us that as we are walking in faith, standing firm on the word of promise God gave us, we're going to face strong opposition from the enemy as well as from people around us — even from family and friends at times. That's why you have to resolve that you will never bend, break, or surrender. Instead, you're going to maintain the word God gave you and see it come to pass.

The Trouble Paul Experienced Was Unparalleled and Beyond His Ability To Endure

A great example of standing in faith amidst overwhelming opposition is found in Paul's second letter to the Corinthians where he said, "For we would not, brethren, have you ignorant of our trouble which came to us in Asia, that we were pressed out of measure, above strength, insomuch that we despaired even of life" (2 Corinthians 1:8).

First, Paul told the believers in Corinth he didn't want them to be "ignorant" — *uninformed of the facts* — of the "trouble" he had experienced in Asia. Interestingly, the word "trouble" is the Greek word *thlipsis*, which is the same word we saw translated as "afflictions" in Hebrews 10:33. It describes *affliction, tribulation,* or *trouble*. It portrays *a situation so difficult it produces great pressure; crushing pressure; suffocating pressure;* or *a horribly tight, life-threatening squeeze*.

Paul said the trouble he was in caused him to feel "pressed out of measure." This phrase is a translation of the Greek word *huperballo*, which is a compound of the words *huper* and *ballo*. The word *huper* describes *something that is exceeding,* and the word *ballo* means *to throw*. When these words are compounded to form *huperballo*, it describes *something that is above and beyond what is normal; something exceeding or surpassing*. It is the picture of an archer who aims his arrow at the bullseye, but shoots way over the top. Hence, it depicts *something beyond the range of anything considered normal; something unparalleled*.

Not only were Paul and his associates pressed out of measure, he said they were pressed "above strength," which in Greek describes *an experience way beyond one's power and abilities to endure or to overcome.* It's interesting that in the original Greek, it includes the words "weighed down" — which don't appear in the *King James Version.* These words "weighed down" are a translation of the Greek word *bareo,* which means *to weigh down* or *to overload.* It's taken from the word *baros,* which depicts *a weight that is heavy or crushing.* This word could also refer to *a physical problem, circumstantial problem, or spiritual problem.*

Paul inserted the word *bareo* in the original Greek to tell us that what he went through in Asia was beyond anything he had ever experienced before — it was too much for one person to ever bear by himself. In fact, the pressure he experienced was so crushing that he and his associates "…despaired even of life" (2 Corinthians 1:8). The word "despaired" here is the Greek word *exaporeomai,* which describes *a person who feels there is no way out.* He or she feels *trapped, caught, up against a wall, pinned down, and hence, utterly hopeless.*

Paul Put All His Trust in God To Deliver Him

To all this, Paul added, "But we had the sentence of death in ourselves, that we should not trust in ourselves, but in God which raiseth the dead: Who delivered us from so great a death, and doth deliver: in whom we trust that he will yet deliver us" (2 Corinthians 1:9,10). The word "sentence" in verse 9 is the Greek word *apokrima,* and it describes *a judicial rendering; a judicial decision; a final outcome; a final verdict.*

Essentially, Paul and his ministry team members had experienced *a horribly tight, life-threatening squeeze.* But as crushing as the circumstances were and as hard as the enemy came against him, God preserved the lives of Paul and his associates. And just as they experienced the resurrection power of God in their lives, so will you — as long as you stay in your place of faith, doing what God called you to do.

Taking into account the original Greek meaning of all of these words, here is the *Renner Interpretive Version (RIV)* of Second Corinthians 1:8-10:

> **We would not, brothers, have you ignorant of the horribly tight, life-threatening squeeze that came to us in Asia. With all the things we've been through, this was the worst of all — it felt like our lives were being crushed. No experience we've ever**

been through required so much of us. In fact, we didn't have enough strength to cope with it and we were nearly crushed by the experience. Toward the end of this ordeal, we were so overwhelmed that we didn't think we'd ever get out! We felt suffocated, trapped, and pinned against the wall. We really thought it was the end of the road for us! As far as we were concerned, the verdict was in, and the verdict said "death." But really, this was no great shock, because we already were feeling the effect of death.

In our next lesson, we will focus on how your decision to stand in faith will bring the applause of God Himself.

STUDY QUESTIONS

> **Study to shew thyself approved unto God, a workman that needeth not to be ashamed, rightly dividing the word of truth.**
> **— 2 Timothy 2:15**

The apostle Paul said the trouble he and his team experienced in Asia was *something beyond the range of anything considered normal* — a situation *way beyond one's power to endure and overcome.* The circumstances they faced were so hopeless, they even "despaired of life," which means he felt trapped in an inescapable situation.

1. Can you identify with Paul? What circumstances are you currently facing that seem to be unparalleled, inescapable, and beyond the range of anything considered normal?

2. How does it encourage you to know that even Paul — the man who wrote nearly half of the New Testament — felt so overwhelmed at times?

3. What promises does God make in the following verses about going through hard times, and how do they give you a sense of hope?
   - **1 Corinthians 10:13**
   - **Psalm 34:6,7,17-19**
   - **2 Timothy 4:18**
   - **2 Peter 2:9**
   - **Hebrews 13:5,6**

- **Isaiah 43:1-3**
- **Job 5:19**
- **Psalm 91**

PRACTICAL APPLICATION

But be ye doers of the word, and not hearers only,
deceiving your own selves.
—James 1:22

1. What thoughts and feelings well up in your heart when you pause and remember the early days just after you first came to Jesus? What *word* or *phrase* would you use to describe that priceless time when you first began your walk with the Lord?

2. Can you think of a time in your life when the Holy Spirit "illuminated" you concerning a specific truth from God's Word? What was it about? Healing? Protection? Provision? Giving? What scriptures did He make real, and how were your eyes finally opened to understand and see things clearly? What struggles or fears were eliminated from your life as a result?

3. The devil hates people who are illuminated and walking in faith, because illuminated people help bring illumination to others. Who do you know that brought illumination to your life? How did their walk of faith turn on the lights for you? Whose life is being affected by the illumination God has given you? How are they being impacted?

LESSON 4

TOPIC

Your Faith Will Bring Applause

SCRIPTURES

1. **1 Corinthians 4:1-5** — Let a man so account of us, as of the ministers of Christ, and stewards of the mysteries of God. Moreover it is required in stewards, that a man be found faithful. But with me it is a very small thing that I should be judged of you, or of man's judgment: yea, I judge

not mine own self. For I know nothing by myself; yet am I not hereby justified: but he that judgeth me is the Lord. Therefore judge nothing before the time, until the Lord come, who both will bring to light the hidden things of darkness, and will make manifest the counsels of the hearts: and then shall every man have praise of God.

GREEK WORDS

1. "ministers" — ὑπηρέτης (*huperetes*): a class of criminals that were so low, so detestable, and so contemptible, that they were outcast, removed from society, and placed into the bottom galleys of huge ships, where they literally became the engines of ships; they endlessly rowed to keep the ship moving forward; it can be translated minister, servant, or under-rower; depicts individuals who keep things moving; was used to describe an official in a synagogue whose function was to keep things moving; describes one whose will is to fulfill the purpose of his master

2. "stewards" — οἰκονόμος (*oikonomos*): the rule or management of a house; in the Old Testament Greek Septuagint, depicts leaders so trusted by the king or state that they were appointed to administrate entire departments or nations; in secular documents, it is translated court officials or palace officials, and it depicted those entrusted with a public office; household administrators who were entrusted with managerial responsibility to run a house or business in an orderly fashion and according to the rules set forth by the owner

3. "required" — ζητέω (*zeteo*): to seek, to search, or to look very intensively; a legal term to denote a judicial investigation; could refer to a scientific investigation; denotes an intense and thorough searching for accurate, concrete facts, not a mere surface investigation; to search for thoroughly and exhaustively

4. "found" — εὑρίσκω (*heurisko*): to find or to discover; a moment when one makes a surprising or conclusive discovery; it usually points to a discovery made due to an intense investigation, scientific study, or scholarly research

5. "faithful" — πιστός (*pistos*): faithful; dependable; reliable; trustworthy

6. "small thing" — ἐλάχιστος (*elachistos*): the least, the very smallest, absolutely inconsequential

7. "judged" — ἀνακρίνω (*anakrino*): examined; examined again and again; thoroughly examined; forensically examined; a tortuous examination

8. "before" — πρό (*pro*): before; earlier

9. "judge" — κρίνω (*krino*): a legal term meaning to make a decision on the basis of information, like a jury who has heard all the evidence and now possesses all the information needed to produce a decision; an intelligent conclusion based on some type of evidence

10. "will bring to light" — φωτίζω (*photidzo*): to lighten up, to shine, to illuminate; the impression of a brilliant flash of light that leaves a permanent and lasting impression

11. "hidden" — τὰ κρυπτὰ (*ta krupta*): from κρυπτός (*kruptos*), the secret things; outwardly unobservable things; things that are concealed

12. "darkness" — σκότος (*skotos*): denotes physical or spiritual darkness; metaphorically depicts a person, society, world, or spiritual realm that is filled with dark hidden agendas and motives

13. "manifest" — φανερόω (*phaneroo*): to appear, to manifest, to become visible; to become apparent; to become seen; to be well known; or to become conspicuous; to become visible, observable, obvious, clear, open, apparent, or evident

14. "counsels" — τὰς βουλὰς (*tas boulas*): plural, counsels; from βουλή (*boule*), deeply laid plans; counsels; purposes; motives

15. "then" — τότε (*tote*): exactly and precisely at that moment

16. "every man" — ἕκαστος (*hekastos*): an all-inclusive term that embraces everyone, with no one excluded

17. "praise" — ἔπαινος (*epainos*): applause; a round of applause or a standing ovation in response to a performance

SYNOPSIS

One of the most interesting facts about the in-home theater inside the Yusupov Palace in Saint Petersburg, Russia, is the list of some of the high-profile individuals who attended the performances. Not only did the Yusupovs invite friends, ambassadors, and family members, but they also invited royalty — including members of the distinguished Romanov family who were their relatives.

This remarkable theater, which was able to seat up to 180 guests, featured a number of private boxes, including one that was called the incognito box. It was in this small section of seating that Czar (Tsar) Nicholas II would come and recline and enjoy many of the Yusupov's performances. The reason he chose the incognito box was because it was right by the buffet, and the short distance enabled him to sneak out during a performance to get food.

It is actually quite amazing who will show up to watch a performance. And what is true of the natural theater is also true of the spiritual theater. As we've seen, when you are illuminated by God and declare you're going to do something for Him, people will come to watch and see if you're going to accomplish what you said. Out of all the spectators that come, there is one that shows up who is more important than all the others, and that Person is God Himself.

The emphasis of this lesson:

God is searching for faithful ministers and stewards for His Church. For all those who perform their walk of faith with excellence, God Himself will stand to His feet and give them a round of applause. Don't worry about or listen to the judgment of others. Only God is your Judge.

Being faithful to obediently complete what God has called you to accomplish really gets His attention. The truth is, in everything you do, you are ultimately performing for an audience of One. It really doesn't matter what other people think or say about you. It is God's opinion and assessment that matter most. Writing to the believers in Corinth — and to followers of Christ in all generations — the apostle Paul expounds on this truth saying,

> **Let a man so account of us, as of the ministers of Christ, and stewards of the mysteries of God.**
>
> **Moreover it is required in stewards, that a man be found faithful.**
>
> **But with me it is a very small thing that I should be judged of you, or of man's judgment: yea, I judge not mine own self.**
>
> **For I know nothing by myself; yet am I not hereby justified: but he that judgeth me is the Lord.**
>
> **Therefore judge nothing before the time, until the Lord come, who both will bring to light the hidden things of darkness, and will make manifest the counsels of the hearts: and then shall every man have praise of God.**
>
> **1 Corinthians 4:1-5**

There's so much for us to learn in this passage, so let's back up to the first verse and begin to unpack each truth one by one.

Paul Identified Himself as a 'Minister' and 'Steward' of the Mysteries of God

Paul begins his teaching by saying, "Let a man so account of us, as of the ministers of Christ, and stewards of the mysteries of God" (1 Corinthians 4:1). At first glance, you may think the word "ministers" is referring to a man or woman of God wearing a suit or collar who teaches the Word, but it is not.

This word "ministers" is the Greek word *huperetes*, and it depicted *a class of criminals that were so low, so detestable, and so contemptible, that they were outcasts*. These individuals were removed from society, and placed into the bottom galleys of huge ships, where they literally became the engines of ships. They endlessly rowed and kept the ship moving forward. Although this word *huperetes* can also be translated as *minister* or *servant*, it literally describes *an under-rower* and depicts *individuals who keep things moving*. It was even used to describe an official in a synagogue whose function was to keep things moving. Ultimately, it depicts one whose will is to fulfill the purpose of his master.

Paul's use of this word *huperetes* — translated here as "ministers" — is the equivalent of him saying, "We are like the engines of the Gospel ship, and it is our job to make sure that the Church keeps making forward progress." The reason Paul told this to the Corinthian believers is because they glamorized ministry — much like many believers have done today. He wanted them to understand that a true minister of the Gospel is like the ones condemned to the bottom of a ship with the arduous and endless task of keeping it moving forward. If ministers stop doing their job, the Church will stop making forward progress — it's that simple.

In addition to being ministers of Christ, Paul said he and his team members were "…stewards of the mysteries of God" (1 Corinthians 4:1). The word "stewards" here is the Greek word *oikonomos*, which is a compound of the words *oikos* and *nomos*. The word *oikos* is the word for a *house*, and the word *nomos* is the word for *law*. When these words are compounded to form *oikonomos*, it describes *the rule or management of a house* — or even a nation.

In the Old Testament Greek Septuagint, it depicts *leaders so trusted by the king or state* that they were appointed to administrate entire departments or nations. In secular documents, it is translated as *court officials* or *palace officials*, and it depicted *those entrusted with a public office.* These people would have included administrators of cities, states, or nations. Moreover, the word *oikonomos* — translated here as "stewards" — also depicted *household administrators who were entrusted with managerial responsibility to run a house or business in an orderly fashion and according to the rules set forth by the owner.*

Without question, those who were "stewards" were on the public stage, and this is what Paul said Church leaders are like. So while "ministers" of the Gospel were similar to the often forgotten "under rowers" of the Church ship, Paul said they were also people who were highly visible in the public eye. God had entrusted them with the responsibility and task of managing and running the Church in an orderly fashion, and they were to do it according to the rules He had set forth.

God Is Searching for Faithful Stewards

In First Corinthians 4:2, Paul went on to say, "Moreover it is required in stewards, that a man be found faithful." The word "required" here is actually a poor translation. It is the Greek word *zeteo*, and it means *to seek, to search*, or *to look very intensively.* It is a legal term to denote *a judicial investigation*, and could even refer to *a scientific investigation.* It denotes an intense and thorough searching for accurate, concrete facts, *not* a mere surface investigation. It carries the idea of *searching thoroughly and exhaustively for something.*

The use of this word *zeteo* — translated here as "required" — means that God is making a concentrated effort to *look for, search for*, and *investigate* to find stewards and ministers who are faithful. The fact that He is searching so intensely lets us know that these kinds of faithful people are few and far between.

This brings us to the word "found," which is the Greek word *heurisko*, and it means *to find* or *to discover.* It pictures *a moment when one makes a surprising or conclusive discovery.* It usually points to a discovery made due to *an intense investigation, scientific study*, or *scholarly research.* This word *heurisko* — translated here as "found" — is from where we get the word *eureka.*

Friend, when God finds someone who sticks with his or her assignment, stays on the stage of faith, and refuses to budge, He arrives at a moment when He Himself says, "Eureka! I've really found someone who's going to do what I've asked them to do! After My exhaustive investigation and the testing I've administered, I've discovered a person who is truly faithful!" This word "faithful" is the Greek word *pistos*, and it means *faithful, dependable, reliable,* and *trustworthy*. In order for God to place a man or a woman as a manager or administrator in His Church, they are required to be found faithful.

God Is the Judge...
The Judgment of Others Is Inconsequential

When we come to the very next verse in Paul's letter, he switches gears and begins to talk about judging and being judged. He said, "But with me it is a very small thing that I should be judged of you, or of man's judgment: yea, I judge not mine own self" (1 Corinthians 4:3).

The phrase "small thing" in Greek is the word *elachistos*, which means *the least, the very smallest,* or something that is *absolutely inconsequential*. Paul said, "It is absolutely inconsequential that I'm judged by you." The word "judged" here is the Greek word *anakrino*, which is a compound of the words *ana* and *krino*. The word *krino* means *to judge*. But when the word *ana* is attached to the front, it carries the idea of *being examined again and again*. It means to be *thoroughly examined* or *forensically examined; a tortuous examination*. The reason Paul made this statement is because he knew there were people who were forensically examining him — painstakingly dissecting every move he made. They had formed opinions about Paul, and they were spreading them around. But it didn't affect him in the least.

If you really stop to think about it, when someone is performing on the stage and giving it their all, they're not thinking about the people in the audience. On the contrary, that singer or musician or actor is totally focused on themselves, thinking about and concentrating on how well they are performing. That's the way Paul lived his life. He didn't care about what the Corinthian believers — or what anyone else — thought or said about him. He wasn't even concerned about his own heart judging and condemning him. Instead, he was focused on his performance — doing to the best of his ability what God told him to do.

Paul continued, "For I know nothing by myself; yet am I not hereby justified: but he that judgeth me is the Lord" (1 Corinthians 4:4). Basically, Paul said, "I know I'm giving my very best, and I'm not going to tear myself to pieces in the process of trying to walk out my faith assignment. One of these days the Lord will come, and He will judge me and deal with me, but right now I'm focused on performing."

This way of thinking is very important for you to understand and adapt in your own life. Don't allow the judgment and opinions of others to shake you and push you off the stage of faith. If you listen to what others say you will not perform well. Likewise, don't be too hard on yourself. Just focus on what you're called to do. If you've done something wrong, the Holy Spirit will show you. Repent of any sin He reveals (*see* 1 John 1:9), receive His grace (*see* James 4:6) to self-correct your actions, and then go on performing.

Don't Judge Anything or Anyone Prematurely

In First Corinthians 4:5, Paul follows up by saying, "Therefore judge nothing before the time, until the Lord come, who both will bring to light the hidden things of darkness, and will make manifest the counsels of the hearts: and then shall every man have praise of God."

Again, we see the word "judge" — the Greek word *krino*. It is a legal term meaning *to make a decision on the basis of information*, like a jury who has heard all the evidence and now possesses all the information needed to produce a final decision. This word *krino* depicts *an intelligent conclusion based on some type of evidence*. What Paul is telling us here is, "Don't judge anything or anyone prematurely. Wait until all the facts are gathered and revealed." And all the facts will not be in until "the time" the Lord comes again.

God Will Bring All Hidden Things Into the Light

In that moment, the Bible says He "…will bring to light the hidden things of darkness…" (1 Corinthians 4:5). The phrase "will bring to light" is a translation of the Greek word *photidzo* — the same word we saw translated as "illuminated" in Hebrews 10:32. It means *to lighten up, to shine*, or *to illuminate*. It depicts *a brilliant flash of light that leaves a permanent and lasting impression*. The use of this word *photidzo* is the equivalent of Paul saying, "When Jesus comes, the lights are going to be turned on. And in that moment, everything is going to be exposed, allowing everyone to see everything clearly — even things that have been hidden in darkness."

The word "hidden" in First Corinthians 4:5 is from the Greek word *kruptos*, which describes *the secret things*. These are *outwardly unobservable things; things that are concealed* in darkness. The word "darkness" is the Greek word *skotos*, and it denotes *physical or spiritual darkness*. Metaphorically, it depicts a person, society, world, or spiritual realm that is filled with dark, hidden agendas and motives. This verse lets us know that whatever is wrong, the Lord Himself will reveal it.

In fact, the Bible says He "…will make manifest the counsels of the hearts…" (1 Corinthians 4:5). This word "manifest" is very important. It is the Greek word *phaneroo*, which means *to appear, to manifest, to become visible*, or *to become apparent*. It could also be translated *to become seen, to be well known*, or *to become conspicuous*. It carries the idea of becoming *visible, observable, obvious, clear, open, apparent*, or *evident*.

What is the Lord making visible, obvious, and clear? Paul said the "counsels of the hearts." The word "counsels" is taken from the Greek words *tas boulas*, which is plural, meaning *counsels*. It is derived from the word *boule*, which describes *deeply laid plans, counsels, purposes*, or *motives*. When the Lord comes, everything will be made crystal clear. There will be no misunderstanding of the facts, because they will be evident for all to see.

The Faithful Will Be Applauded By God Himself

The apostle Paul concludes verse 5 by saying, "…Then shall every man have praise of God" (1 Corinthians 4:5). The word "then" is the Greek word *tote*, which indicates *exactly* and *precisely at that moment*. The words "every man" are a translation of the Greek word *hekastos*, which is an all-inclusive term that embraces *everyone, with no one excluded*.

Lastly, we have the word "praise," and it is from the Greek word *epainos*, which is the word for *applause*. It signifies *a round of applause* or *a standing ovation* in response to a performance. Thus, a better translation of this part of the verse would be, "Then every single person, no one excluded, will have God's applause in response to their performance."

In our final lesson of this series, we will focus on the reward that awaits you for being faithful to what God called you to do.

STUDY QUESTIONS

**Study to shew thyself approved unto God, a workman that needeth
not to be ashamed, rightly dividing the word of truth.**
— 2 Timothy 2:15

1. God is searching for "faithful" people to serve in all areas of the
    Church. These are individuals who are *faithful, dependable, reliable,*
    and *trustworthy.* If you were to be raptured into Heaven today and
    stand before God's throne, do you think He would categorize you
    as a "faithful" or "unfaithful" servant? On what grounds do you base
    your answer? Since you still have the opportunity, what about your life
    would you change?

2. What powerful promise does Jesus Himself make to you about *faith-
    fulness* in Matthew 25:21,23 (also in Mark 13:34)?

3. Judgment doesn't only come from others — it often comes from
    ourselves. Our own conscience rises up and begins to condemn us and
    declare us guilty. Have you experienced this? Carefully reflect on what
    the Holy Spirit spoke through the apostle John in First John 3:19,20
    (*AMPC*).

4. "By this we shall come to know (perceive, recognize, and understand)
    that we are of the Truth, and can reassure (quiet, conciliate, and pac-
    ify) our hearts in His presence, whenever our hearts in [tormenting]
    self-accusation make us feel guilty and condemn us. [For we are in
    God's hands.] For He is above and greater than our consciences (our
    hearts), and He knows (perceives and understands) everything [noth-
    ing is hidden from Him.]"

5. What is God speaking to you through this passage? How do these
    words bring you peace?

PRACTICAL APPLICATION

But be ye doers of the word, and not hearers only,
deceiving your own selves.
— James 1:22

1. Paul was surrounded by numerous critics who were judging and
    scrutinizing everything he did. But he learned to ignore their insults
    and attacks and live his life focusing on his performance. Are there
    people you know who are dissecting your every move and spewing

their harsh opinions? Have you allowed their judgment and opinions to shake you and push you off the stage of faith?

2. God and God alone is your judge. He is the only One who sees and understands every single detail of your life — including the motives behind every word you speak and the actions you take. How does this truth encourage you and help you deal with the criticism of others?

3. If you've done something wrong, the Holy Spirit will show you. If He has revealed sin in your life, receive His conviction and follow these steps in God's Word: Repent of any sin He reveals (*see* 1 John 1:9); receive His grace (*see* James 4:6) to self-correct your actions, and then go on performing.

LESSON 5

TOPIC

Your Faith Will Bring You Rewards

SCRIPTURES

1. **Hebrews 10:32,33** — But call to remembrance the former days, in which, after ye were illuminated, ye endured a great fight of afflictions; partly, whilst ye were made a gazingstock both by reproaches and afflictions; and partly, whilst ye became companions of them that were so used.

2. **Hebrews 10:35-39** — Cast not away therefore your confidence, which hath great recompence of reward. For ye have need of patience, that, after ye have done the will of God, ye might receive the promise. For yet a little while, and he that shall come will come, and will not tarry. Now the just shall live by faith: but if any man draw back, my soul shall have no pleasure in him. But we are not of them who draw back unto perdition; but of them that believe to the saving of the soul.

GREEK WORDS

1. "but" — δὲ (*de*): an exclamatory point

2. "call to remembrance" — ἀναμιμνήσκω (*anamimnesko*): to recollect; to unbury, dust off, resurrect, and remember

3. "former" — **πρότερον** (*proteron*): former; before; earlier

4. "illuminated" — **φωτίζω** (*photidzo*): to lighten up, to shine, to illuminate; the impression of a brilliant flash of light that leaves a permanent and lasting impression

5. "endured" — **ὑπομένω** (*hupomeno*): to stay or abide; to remain in one's spot; to keep a position; to resolve to maintain territory gained; in a military sense, it pictures soldiers ordered to maintain their positions even in the face of opposition; to defiantly stick it out regardless of pressures mounted against it; staying power; hang-in-there power; the attitude that holds out, holds on, outlasts, perseveres, and hangs in there, never giving up, refusing to surrender to obstacles, and turning down every opportunity to quit; it pictures one who is under a heavy load but refuses to bend, break, or surrender because he is convinced that the territory, promise, or principle under assault rightfully belongs to him

6. "great" — **πολλὴν** (*pollen*): great in terms of quantity; many; substantial numbers

7. "fight" — **ἄθλησις** (*athlesis*): an athletic term that refers to the attitude and activities of a committed athlete; denotes athletic competitions or athletic games; can be translated as the word struggle; denotes a heroic act

8. "afflictions" — **πάθημα** (*pathema*): suffering; a strong emotional struggle; emotional or mental agony

9. "gazingstock" — **θεατρίζω** (*theatridzo*): theater; to observe, to watch, to study, to scrutinize, or to bring upon the stage for all to see; pictures spectators in the theater watching a scenario being played before them; on the edge of their seats, spectators wait for the actors to make a mistake or forget a line so they can scorn, ridicule him, and make fun of him; it can be interpreted to bring on to the stage in order to scorn, to scoff at, to shame, sneer at, and to publicly humiliate; spectacle

10. "cast" — **ἀποβάλλω** (*apoballo*): to throw away; to discard; or to get rid of something no longer desired, needed, or wanted

11. "confidence" — **παρρησία** (*parresia*): a bold, frank, forthright speech; confidence; audacious; emboldened; extraordinarily frank; a daring to speak what one believes or thinks with no hesitation or concern, possibly even in the face of retribution; boldness; assurance; unashamed confidence; frankness of speech that accompanies unflinching authority

12. "great" — **μεγάλην** (*megalen*): speaks of enormity

13. "recompense of reward" — **μισθαποδοσία** (*misthapodosia*): money, salary, or a payment that is due; primarily used to denote a payment, salary, or reward given for a job performed; can describe a recompense, reimbursement, settlement, or reparation; being reimbursed for an expense a person has paid out of his own pocket in order to get his job done; a full and complete recompense

14. "need" — **χρεία** (*chreia*): a deficit; a need that must be met

15. "patience" — **ὑπομονή** (*hupomone*): to stay or to abide; to remain in one's spot; to keep a position; to resolve to maintain territory that has been gained; in a military sense to picture soldiers who were ordered to maintain their positions even in the face of fierce combat; to defiantly stick it out regardless of the pressure mounted against it; endurance; staying power; hang-in-there power; the attitude that holds out, holds on, outlasts, perseveres, and hangs in there, never giving up, refusing to surrender to obstacles, and turning down every opportunity to quit; it pictures one who is under a heavy load but refuses to bend, break, or surrender because he is convinced that the territory, promise, or principle under assault rightfully belongs to him; stamina, durability

16. "done" — **ποιέω** (*poieo*): to do; to creatively do; involves effort and creativity

17. "receive" — **κομίζω** (*komidzo*): to receive; to receive what is due; to receive what one has coming to him

18. "tarry" — **χρονίζω** (*chronidzo*): time; season; to be in proper sequence or timing

19. "draw back" — **ὑποστέλλω** (*hupostello*): shrink back; one who is withdrawing, retreating, regressing, receding, backing away, backsliding, or recoiling from something; one who reverses his direction; to move backward instead of forward; to back off and retreat from an object, principle, or task

20. "perdition" — **ἀπώλεια** (*apoleia*): something so ruined and rotten that it is decomposing; describes the stench of a decaying animal or a dead human body; a loathsome, putrid, vulgar, disgusting, nauseating scent; something in the process of perishing; doomed, rotten, ruinous, or decaying

SYNOPSIS

As we have noted previously, the in-home theater in the Yusupov Palace in Saint Petersburg, Russia, was truly a remarkable place. There were notable people that came to watch, and notable people that came to perform. Chopin, Liszt, and many other famous musicians and singers of that time took center stage and displayed their divine gifts and callings for all who assembled.

In a similar way, when you make a declaration of faith, you are moved out of the shadows and into the spotlight of center stage. Until that moment, your life was likely quiet, but once you were illuminated by God and you stepped out in faith to fulfill the assignment He gave you, people began watching you perform. And since people love a good show, you should do your best to give them a great presentation.

What has God asked you to do? What dream or assignment has He placed in your heart? Is it to start a business? Write a book? Go into ministry? Begin a musical career? Remodel your house? Get married and raise a family? Or go back to school and earn a special degree? What are you believing Him to do through you? Whatever your assignment or dream is, it is significant. And if you'll be faithful to perform well to the end and do what God has placed in your heart, your life will have a rippling effect on many others, and your faith will bring you a reward.

The emphasis of this lesson:

God warns us not to cast away our confidence in Him or His promises. He wants us to hold tightly to our faith, allowing His supernatural patience to develop in us. Payday is coming! And we will receive a full reward if we choose to trust what He said and refuse to draw back.

A Final Review of Our Anchor Verses
Hebrews 10:32,33

As we saw in Lessons 1 and 3, the Bible says, "But call to remembrance the former days, in which, after ye were illuminated, ye endured a great fight of afflictions; partly, whilst ye were made a gazingstock both by reproaches and afflictions; and partly, whilst ye became companions of them that were so used." To fully grasp the meaning of these verses, let's review the key words in this passage once more.

First, we saw that the word "but" is the Greek word *de*, and here it is like *an exclamatory point*. Remember, the writer of Hebrews was writing to a group of believers that were struggling in their faith. They had been standing in faith for a long time — performing, believing, and waiting for God to answer their prayers. But their requests had still not been answered, and they had grown weary in the wait. As a result, they were tempted to throw away their faith. And just as they were about to step off the stage and walk away from their assignment, the writer of Hebrews said, "Hey, wait! Stop! There's something you need to remember." That's what the word "but" — the Greek word *de* — means.

"But call to remembrance the former days…" (Hebrews 10:32). The phrase "call to remembrance" is a translation of a single Greek word, the word *anamimnesko*. It means *to recollect; to unbury, dust off, resurrect, and remember*. In the process of time, our hopes and dreams and the things God has instructed us to do often get buried by disappointments, adverse circumstances, and the negativity and cynicism of others who oppose us. This is what happened to the First-Century believers the writer of Hebrews was speaking to. That is why he told them to *remember the former days*.

The word "former" is the Greek word *proteron*, which means *former, before,* or *earlier*. The writer then specified that these *earlier days* were when these believers had been "illuminated." We've seen that the word "illuminated" is from the Greek word *photidzo*, which is from where we get the word *photograph*. It means *to lighten up, to shine,* or *to illuminate*. It depicts *a brilliant flash of light that leaves a permanent and lasting impression*. The day you were "illuminated" would be a moment in the past when the Lord suddenly gave you a powerful revelation of truth. It was as if He turned on the lights regarding a specific truth in His Word or the calling on your life. That moment was so enlightening it left a permanent, lasting impression that transformed you.

An "illuminated" person possesses the power to change lives. That is why the devil comes against us so fiercely after we have been "illuminated." He uses everything at his disposal to discourage us, scare us, and deplete us of our health and resources in order to push us off of the stage of faith and quit performing. That's what the enemy did to the early Hebrew believers, and it's why the writer noted that they had "…endured a great fight of afflictions…" (Hebrews 10:32).

To "endure" means *to defiantly stick it out regardless of pressures mounted against it.* This word "endured" is a translation of the Greek word *hupomeno*, which means *to stay or abide; to remain in one's spot; to keep a position;* or *to resolve to maintain territory gained.* In a military sense, it pictures soldiers ordered to maintain their positions even in the face of opposition. It could be translated as *staying power* or *hang-in-there power.* It is *the attitude that holds out, holds on, outlasts, perseveres, and hangs in there, never giving up, refusing to surrender to obstacles, and turning down every opportunity to quit.* Furthermore, the word *hupomeno* — translated here as "endured" — pictures one who is under a heavy load but refuses to bend, break, or surrender because he is convinced that the territory, promise, or principle under assault rightfully belongs to him. Why? Because God has illuminated him.

At times we're confronted by "great afflictions" from life, from people, and from the enemy. The Bible says the Hebrew believers endured "a great fight of afflictions." We've noted that the word "great" is the Greek word *pollen*, which describes *something great in terms of quantity.* It can also indicate *many* or *substantial numbers.* The word "fight" in Greek is the word *athlesis*, which is an athletic term that refers to *the attitude and activities of a committed athlete.* Equally important, it describes *a heroic act.* This tells us that to do what God has called us to do we have to make the decision to be heroic even if we have to deal with "afflictions."

The word "afflictions" in Hebrews 10:32 is a translation of the Greek word *pathema*, and it describes *suffering.* This word could also be translated as *a strong emotional struggle* or *emotional or mental agony.* It is the kind of suffering Jesus faced in the Garden of Gethsemane the night He was betrayed. The mental and emotional anguish He endured was so great He literally sweat drops of blood (*see* Luke 22:44). The truth is, the most difficult part of suffering is not what you feel in your body — it's what you experience in your mind and your emotions. This is the area the devil always attacks. If you can learn how to submit yourself to God and take control over your mind, you can conquer anything.

When you're standing in faith, you become a theatrical performance that others watch. In Hebrews 10:33, the Bible says, "…Ye were made a gazingstock both by reproaches and afflictions; and partly, whilst ye became companions of them that were so used." This word "gazingstock" is the Greek word *theatridzo*, which is the word for a *theater.* It means *to observe, to watch, to study, to scrutinize, or to bring upon the stage for all to see.*

It pictures spectators in the theater watching a scenario being played out before them. They're on the edge of their seats, like spectators waiting for the actors to make a mistake or forget a line so they can scorn, ridicule, and make fun of them.

This word *theatridzo* — translated here as "gazingstock" — can also be interpreted *to bring on to the stage in order to scorn, to scoff at, to shame, sneer at, and to publicly humiliate*. It is often translated as the word *spectacle*, which tells us that when you make a declaration of faith, you become a *big show* and the subject of people's conversations. It's as if people buy a ticket to sit and watch you perform. "Will he actually do what he said God called him to do," they say. They are gazing at you to see if you'll accomplish things like finish school, start a business, get married, launch out into ministry, or write that book you've talked about.

Like it or not, the moment you make a declaration of faith and step out in obedience and partner with God to see it become a reality, you become a "gazingstock" or a *theater* that people observe. Ironically, when you reach the end of your performance and you've done well with what you set out to do, the same people who criticized you and forensically examined your every move will be the same individuals who will stand up and give you a round of applause.

Cast Not Away Your Confidence

Just after the writer of Hebrews explained how we become a "gazingstock," he took time again to encourage his readers who were really struggling in their faith not to give up. Specifically, he said, "Cast not away therefore your confidence, which hath great recompence of reward" (Hebrews 10:35).

The word "cast" in this verse is a translation of the Greek word *apoballo*, which is a compound of the word *apo*, meaning *away*, and the word *ballo*, meaning *to throw*. When these words are combined to form the word *apoballo*, it means *to throw away, to discard*, or *to get rid of something no longer desired, needed, or wanted*. This same word *apoballo* is used in Mark 10:50 in the story of blind Bartimaeus when he was trying to get to Jesus.

Apparently, his legs were wrapped with a garment, and that garment was restricting him from getting where he wanted to go. The Bible says, "And he [Bartimaeus], casting away his garment, rose, and came to Jesus." The words "casting away" are a translation of this word *apoballo*. When

Bartimaeus was hindered by the garment wrapped around him, he ripped it off and threw it aside in order to get to Jesus to receive his healing. The writer of Hebrews used this word *apoballo* — translated as "cast not away" — to urge believers **not** to *throw away* or *discard* their confidence.

The use of this word tells us that these believers were likely tempted to think, *Ever since we've received that word of illumination from God, our lives have been hindered and on pause. If we had never gotten that word of instruction, we could have gone on with our lives. But when we heard God speak to us, we chose to stand in faith — believing day after day, year after year that He would do what He said. We've been on the stage of faith for a long time doing our part, but nothing has really happened. People continue to watch us, but our prayers are still not answered. Enough is enough. It's time we take this word of illumination and throw it away so we can move on with our lives.*

In response, the writer of Hebrews urgently pleaded, "Cast not away therefore your confidence…" (Hebrews 10:35). The word "confidence" here is a translation of the Greek word *parresia*, and it describes *a bold, frank, forthright kind of speech*. It depicts *confidence; one that is audacious or emboldened*. It denotes *openness* and carries the idea of being *extraordinarily frank*. It is *daring to speak what one believes or thinks without hesitation or concern — possibly even in the face of retribution*. Furthermore, it indicates *boldness; assurance; unashamed confidence; it is a frankness of speech that accompanies unflinching authority*.

The "confidence" of these Hebrew believers was their *confession of faith*.

The use of the word *parresia* — translated here as "confidence" — tells us that these believers were very bold and audacious in their confession of faith when they began their walk with God. They had been "illuminated" and were standing firm on what God had showed them. But because what they were believing for had not manifested yet, they were tempted to throw it all away as though the manifestation was never going to come to pass.

God's Reward Is on Its Way

What was the reason for not casting away their confidence? The Bible says that maintaining confidence "…hath great recompence of reward" (Hebrews 10:35). The phrase "recompense of reward" is from the Greek word *misthapodosia*, which is the term for *money, salary, or a payment that is due*. It is primarily used to denote *a payment, salary, or reward given for a job performed*. It can also describe *a recompense, reimbursement, settlement, or reparation.* Moreover, it means *to be reimbursed for an expense a person has paid out of his own pocket in order to get his job done; a full and complete recompense.*

Here the writer of Hebrews basically said, "If you will hang on and continue to boldly confess your faith in God, payday is coming! He is going to reimburse you greatly for everything you've given out." The word "great" in this verse speaks of enormity. In other words, God has a magnificent payback coming your way if you'll just hang on.

Then he adds in the next verse, "For ye have need of patience, that, after ye have done the will of God, ye might receive the promise" (Hebrews 10:36).

Although this may have been the last thing this group of believers wanted to hear, it was what they needed to hear. The word "patience" is the Greek word *hupomone*, which is the same word we saw translated as "endured" in verse 32. Again, it means *to stay or to abide; to remain in one's spot;* or *to keep a position.* It is to be *immovable* until the thing prayed for is manifested. It is *the attitude that holds out, holds on, outlasts, perseveres, and hangs in there, never giving up, refusing to surrender to obstacles, and turning down every opportunity to quit.*

In the process of waiting, God's supernatural "patience" (*hupomone*) is developed inside of us. The writer of Hebrews went on to say, "…After ye have done the will of God, ye might receive the promise" (Hebrews 10:36). The word "receive" here is the Greek word *komidzo*, which literally means *to receive what is due* or *to receive what one has coming to him.* The inclusion of this word in this passage is the equivalent of saying, "Whatever promise of God you have been declaring by faith — whatever you have been boldly speaking and believing God for — is coming to you. It is your *recompense* or *reward* that is on its way to you — as long as you don't give up."

The Bible goes on to say, "For yet a little while, and he that shall come will come, and will not tarry" (Hebrews 10:37). The word "little" in this verse is the Greek word *micros*, and it describes *something that is microscopic.* Here the Holy Spirit is encouraging us by letting us know that in a *microscopic* amount of time, the answer we have been praying for and waiting for will come. In other words, what was "illuminated" to us is on its way. It will not "tarry," which in Greek means it will come *in the proper sequence or timing…* as long as we (*hupomone*) hang in there, stay put, and don't quit.

Refuse To 'Draw Back' From Faith
and Choose To Trust What God Has Said

When we come to verse 38, the writer makes this declaration: "Now the just shall live by faith: but if any man draw back, my soul shall have no pleasure in him." Notice the phrase "draw back." It is the Greek word *hupostello*, which means *to shrink back*. It pictures *one who is withdrawing, retreating, regressing, receding, backing away, backsliding, or recoiling from something*. This shrinking back usually takes place gradually, one step at a time. As this person experiences one little discouragement after another, he releases his grip on his "confidence," which is his *confession of faith*. Furthermore, the word *hupostello* depicts *one who reverses his direction*. It carries the idea of *moving backward instead of forward*. It means *to back off and retreat from an object, principle, or task*.

That is what the Hebrew believers were tempted to do. They were thinking things like, *Why should we keep believing and standing in faith? Surely what we're believing for should have happened by now. Our lives have been on hold. We could have moved on, but no! We had to have a word from God and make a declaration of faith. Ever since then, we've been stuck here believing and confessing, believing and confessing. Maybe we should just abandon all of this and move on.*

In response to their internal struggle, the writer of Hebrews immediately added, "But we are not of them who draw back unto perdition; but of them that believe to the saving of the soul" (Hebrews 10:39). Once again, we see the phrase "draw back" — the Greek word *hupostello*. In this case, he is saying, "We are *not* the kind of people that *shrink back, withdraw*, or *retreat* from our position of faith." Specifically, he said, "But we are not of them who draw back unto perdition..." (Hebrews 10:39).

The word "perdition" is the Greek word *apoleia*, and it pictures *something ruined, rotten, and decomposing*. It was used to describe *the stench of a decaying animal or a dead human body*. It denoted *a loathsome, putrid, vulgar, disgusting, nauseating scent; something in the process of perishing; something doomed, rotten, ruinous, or decaying*. This word *apoleia* — translated here as "perdition" — gives us a vivid picture of what happens to people who draw back from their position of faith. When they throw away their faith, they begin to emit a terrible spiritual stench and acquire a nauseating attitude of cynicism and bitterness about life and those who are walking in faith. If you've ever been there, you know how awful this condition can be.

That is why the writer of Hebrews urged his readers — *and us* — to live by *faith*. This word "faith" in Hebrews 10:38 is the Greek word *pistis*, and it describes *a force that is propelling you forward toward a goal*. Its root means *to persuade, to trust,* or *to believe.* It is *a persuasion from God that imparts an impulse or "divine spark" to believe.* When you're in faith, you are moving forward. But when you release or walk away from your faith, you are moving in reverse — you are losing territory and drifting into negativity.

Friend, stay on the stage of faith! Hold tightly to what God has illuminated, and continue to boldly declare His promises. If you'll keep performing and doing what God told you to do — turning a deaf ear to every voice of opposition and rejecting every opportunity to quit — payday is on the way! And when it comes, it will be right on time. In that moment, you will receive the answer to your prayers. Relationships will be restored, deliverance will occur, financial provision will be received, and healing will take place.

STUDY QUESTIONS

Study to shew thyself approved unto God, a workman that needeth not to be ashamed, rightly dividing the word of truth.
— 2 Timothy 2:15

1. The Bible says that *faith* — which is the ability to believe and trust God and His Word — is a gift from God that all of us have received (*see* Romans 12:3; Ephesians 2:8,9). According to Romans 10:17, what should you do regularly to enable your faith to grow? (Also consider Luke 8:15; John 8:31,32; James 1:21.)

2. Can you remember some of the rewards God has given you in the past for faithfully holding on to what He promised? What are they, and which one is the most precious to you?

3. What specifically are you believing God to do in your *marriage*, your *family*, your *business*, your *church*, or your *community*? What related scriptures are you holding on to and confessing out loud in faith?

PRACTICAL APPLICATION

But be ye doers of the word, and not hearers only, deceiving your own selves.
—James 1:22

1. The believers the writer addressed in Hebrews had been waiting and waiting for God to answer their prayers, but they still had not seen any results. Can you identify with their situation? What have you been praying for God to do in your life for a long time that has still not come to pass?

2. To "draw back" from faith means to *withdraw*, *retreat* or *backslide* from what God has spoken. The result of such backsliding is "perdition," which means our lives begin to emit a terrible spiritual stench and develop a nauseating attitude of cynicism and bitterness. Have you or someone you know experienced these symptoms? If so, how would you describe the condition of your/their life and family?

3. Be honest: Have you *drawn back* from your faith in God in a particular area? Are you disappointed or offended with Him over something? If so, explain your situation. What has caused you to spiritually retreat and reverse your direction? Take a few moments to pour out your heart to God, asking Him to forgive you of anything specific He brings to mind. And pray for His grace to get back on the stage of faith and do what He has called you to do.

Notes

Notes

Notes

Notes

_____

_____

_____

_____

_____

_____

_____

_____

_____

_____

_____

_____

_____

_____

_____

_____

_____

_____

_____

_____

_____

_____

_____

_____

_____

_____

_____

_____

_____

Notes

Notes

_____

_____

_____

_____

_____

_____

_____

_____

_____

_____

_____

_____

_____

_____

_____

_____

_____

_____

_____

_____

_____

_____

_____

_____

_____

_____

_____

_____

_____

Notes

Notes

_____

_____

_____

_____

_____

_____

_____

_____

_____

_____

_____

_____

_____

_____

_____

_____

_____

_____

_____

_____

_____

_____

_____

_____

_____

_____

_____

_____

_____

Notes

www.ingramcontent.com/pod-product-compliance
Lightning Source LLC
Chambersburg PA
CBHW051046030426
42339CB00006B/221